THE BILL CLINTON
JOKE BOOK

THE BILL CLINTON
JOKE BOOK

by Mitchell Symons

CHAMELEON

First published in Great Britain in 1998 by
Chameleon Books, an imprint of André Deutsch Ltd
76 Dean Street London W1V 5HA
André Deutsch is a VCI plc company

A catalogue record for this title is available from
the British Library

ISBN 0 233 99438 6

Printed in Great Britain by WBC,
Bridgend, Mid-Glamorgan

To Bill, Hillary and Chelsea – with thanks.
To Penny, Jack and Charlie – with love.

It has always been the proud boast of Americans that anyone can become President of their country. Well, in 1992, 'anyone' just did. And, just to emphasize how easy it is for 'anyone' to become Head of State and Commander-in-Chief of the most powerful country in the world, he was voted back in 1996.

And the American public knew all about – well, pretty well all about – all of Bill Clinton's extra-marital affairs.

Consequently, any joke book is always going to come second to the biggest joke of the lot: the election of this sexual incontinent (and his re-election).

These jokes come from a variety of different sources. I've taken some from newspaper cuttings, some from the Internet and some from joke books. I've been given jokes by friends, colleagues and, with the current fascination with Bill Clinton and his sex life, strangers (like cabbies, shop assistants and, on one memorable occasion, an American who was sitting at the next table in a restaurant). I've even written some forty or fifty jokes myself. They're the ones you read and then say 'I don't see what's funny about that'.

There is one person I must thank for giving me the push start I needed to get this book off the ground. So, thank you, Russell Ash, for your Top Ten (and more) Clinton jokes.

A new sex survey shows that 70% of men remain faithful to their wives. President Clinton was mortified: just once he'd like a poll to go his way.

Al Gore, Dan Quayle, Ross Perot and Bill Clinton all went to meet the Wizard of Oz. First, Al Gore told the Wizard, 'Everyone says I have no feelings, I want to have a Heart.'

The Wizard said, 'So be it.'

Second was Dan Quayle. He said to the Wizard, 'People think I'm unintelligent, I want to have a Brain.'

The Wizard said, 'So be it.'

Third was Ross Perot. 'People say I lack conviction, I want to have Courage.'

The Wizard said, 'So be it.'

Finally, the Wizard noticed Bill Clinton. 'And what do you want?' he asked the President.

'Oh nothing,' replied Clinton. 'I'm here for Dorothy.'

During the 1992 election campaign, Dan Quayle said that if his daughter got pregnant, he'd let her decide whether or not to have an abortion. Marilyn Quayle said that if her daughter got pregnant, she would insist that she have the baby. Bill Clinton said, 'The woman's a liar. I was in New York at the time.'

If you saw Bill Clinton drowning in a river and you had a choice between rescuing him or taking a Pulitzer Prize-winning photograph, what shutter speed would you use?

What would happen if Hillary Clinton got shot?
Bill Clinton would become president.

The Pope postponed all his appointments for a week – just so he could hear Clinton's confession.

The Pope and Clinton die at the same time
– but by mistake Clinton ends up in heaven
and the Pope in hell. As they are both re-
routed, the Pope says how much he's looking
forward to meeting the Virgin Mary. Clinton
replies: 'Sorry, your Holiness, you're too late
by thirty minutes.'

Clinton is consulting a few dead presidents.
When he asks them for their best advice,
George Washington advises 'be honest',
Thomas Jefferson says, 'be strong' and
Abraham Lincoln counsels, 'take Hillary to the
theatre.'

Bill Clinton is doing the work of three men: Curly, Larry and Moe.

Clinton returns from a holiday in Arkansas and walks down the steps of Air Force One with two pigs under his arms. At the bottom of the steps, he says to the guardsman, 'These are genuine Arkansas Razorback Hogs. I got this one for Chelsea and this one for Hillary.' The guardsman replies, 'Nice trade, sir.'

What is Bill Clinton's political philosophy?
If they're too young to vote, fuck 'em.

Bill Clinton got a shock when somebody threw a beer at him. Fortunately, it turned out to be a draft and Clinton was able to dodge it.

Why does Bill Clinton wear boxer shorts?
To keep his ankles warm.

What's Bill Clinton's favourite brand of toothpaste?
Oral B.

What's the most popular game in the White House?
Swallow My Leader.

President Clinton looks up from his desk in the Oval Office to see one of his aides nervously approaching him. 'What is it?' asks the President.

'It's this Abortion Bill, Mr President,' says the aide. 'What do you want to do about it?'

'Just go ahead and pay it,' answers the President.

Bill and Hillary are at the first baseball game of the season. The umpire walks up to the VIP section and says something. Suddenly, Bill grabs Hillary by the collar and throws her over the wall on to the field. The stunned umpire shouts, 'No, Mr President! I said, "throw the first PITCH"!'

Tony Blair and President Clinton are sitting together in the White House. 'Hey, want to hear a good Clinton joke?' asks Blair.

'But *I'm* President Clinton,' says Clinton.

'Oh, that's okay,' says Blair. 'I'll tell it slowly.'

What's the difference between God and Bill Clinton?
God doesn't think he's Bill Clinton.

Bill Clinton has an explanation for the entire scandal: 'Those young interns have big mouths and like to blow things out of all proportion.'

A man died and went to heaven. St Peter met him at the Pearly Gates and told him to come on in. The man went into a room with thousands of clocks. He asked St Peter why all of these clocks were in there. St Peter replied, 'each clock is a person's lies, and we measure everybody's lies by these clocks.'

St Peter showed him Abraham Lincoln's and it had only turned a little, and then Thomas Jefferson's and it had only turned a little, and then George Washington's and it hadn't turned at all. Then the man asked 'Well, where's Bill Clinton's?'

St Peter responded 'It's upstairs, we're using it as a ceiling fan.'

Why did Bill Clinton have to cancel his plans to add his face to Mount Rushmore?
He was told there wasn't room for two more faces.

What's the difference between the last Presidential election and the last Superbowl? In the last Superbowl they *kicked a punt*.

Bill and Hillary are at a restaurant. The waiter tells them that the specials are chicken forestiere and fresh sea bass. 'The chicken sounds good,' says Hillary. 'I'll have that.' The waiter nods.

'And the vegetable?' asks the waiter.

'Oh, he'll have the fish,' Hillary replies.

Bill and Hillary are on a sinking boat. Who gets saved?
The nation.

When asked if he will be able to save his political career, Clinton said, 'It will be all up Hill from now on.'

Hillary Clinton is the only woman to stand by her man.
All the rest had to kneel.

What do Monica Lewinsky and Bob Dole have in common?
They were both upset when Bill finished first.

What is Bill's definition of safe sex?
When Hillary is out of town.

After his liaison with Monica Lewinsky, Bill decided to make it up to Hillary. So he bought her a massive bouquet of red roses. Hillary, delighted, rushed him upstairs and stripped off to reveal exotic lingerie. She then pulled him towards her, opened her legs and whispered, 'This is for the present.'

'What?' replied Bill, 'Haven't you got a vase then?'

What's the difference between Clinton and the Titanic?
Only 200 women went down on the Titanic.

Bill Clinton is guilty of breaking the Eleventh Commandment – the one that goes: 'Thou shalt not put thy rod in thy staff.'

How does Bill keep Monica Lewinsky away from the White House?
He keeps offering to send Ted Kennedy over to give her a ride.

Bill Clinton has released new revelations about his sex life. He's finally admitted that he had sex with Gennifer Flowers a couple of times . . . but he didn't come.

What's Bill Clinton's personal motto?
If one swallow doesn't make a summer, try two.

When did Clinton realize Paula Jones wasn't a Democrat?
When she didn't swallow everything he offered her.

What's the definition of an Arkansas virgin?
A girl that can run faster than the Governor.

Why is Clinton so interested in events in the Middle East?
He thinks the Gaza Strip is a topless bar.

Tony Blair asked Bill Clinton what he thought of the Northern Ireland position.
Clinton replied: 'I haven't tried it yet.'

Bill Clinton was having a hospital operation. When he woke up in the recovery room the curtains were closed and it was very dark. When the doctor came in, Clinton asked him why the room was so dark, to which the doctor replied, 'There was a fire down the road and I didn't want you to come to and think you had died.'

Have you seen the Bill Clinton watch? It has a big hand, a little hand and a wandering hand.

What do you get when you cross a corrupt politician with a lousy lawyer?
Chelsea Clinton.

What's the difference between Liberace and Bill Clinton?
Clinton's not yet been finished off by his aides.

One Friday night, Bill Clinton walked over to the Executive Offices and discovered his young staffers having a wild party. He saw that a white sheet with a hole in it had been strung across one of the offices. A secretary explained, 'The guys take turns sticking their dicks through the hole and we have to guess who they are.'

'Sounds like fun,' said Bill, 'Wish I'd been there.'

'You should have been,' said the secretary, 'Your name came up nine times.'

The President has announced he wants to tell the truth, the whole truth and nothing but the truth. The problem is that for Bill Clinton they're three different things.

Hillary was out walking when she spotted a little boy playing with cow manure. 'Little boy, what are you doing?' she asked.

'I'm making a model of Al Gore,' replied the boy.

'Why are you making Al Gore?' asked

Hillary. 'Why not make a model of Bill Clinton?'

'Oh no, Ma'am, I can't make a model of Bill Clinton.'

'Why not?' asked Hillary.

'There isn't enough bullshit here to make Bill Clinton.'

What do Bill Clinton and a hypodermic syringe have in common?
They're both a pain in the arse.

What does Monica Lewinsky
boast about in her CV?
That she spent eighteen months on the President's staff.

Three teenagers are walking down the street in Washington DC when they see Bill Clinton out jogging. He's crossing the road and they realize that he's going to be hit by a car.

So, without thinking, they pull the President out of the way, thus saving his life. 'Thank you for saving my life, fellas,' says Bill. 'I'm going to give each of you one wish.' The first boy says, 'I want a car.' Bill says he'll arrange it. The second boy says, 'I want a vacation in Florida.' Bill says he'll fix it. The third boy says, 'I want to be buried in Arlington National Cemetery.' Bill says, 'That's a strange request for a sixteen-year-old?' 'Sure,' says the boy, 'but when my father finds out whose life I saved, he's going to kill me!'

Bill Clinton likes to compare himself to John F Kennedy. However, Hillary was recently over-heard telling him, 'JFK died tragically with half a brain after being shot in the head. You haven't even got a bullet to blame.'

How does Bill Clinton fire up his lawyer?
He tells him to go out there and win one for the zipper.

Bill and Hillary are driving through Arkansas when they see one of her old boyfriends pumping petrol at a roadside service station. 'Just think,' says Bill, 'if you had married him instead of me you would never have been First Lady.'

'Wrong,' replies Hillary. 'If I had married him instead of you I would STILL be First Lady but HE would have been President.'

Bumper Sticker: WHERE THE HELL IS LEE HARVEY OSWALD NOW THAT WE REALLY NEED HIM?

Bill Clinton considers his looks to be a cross between Paul Newman and Robert Redford. Apparently, both stars are undergoing extensive plastic surgery.

Bill Clinton dies and goes to Heaven where he's asked who he is and what he did. Bill replies, 'I am Bill Clinton, and I was President of the United States.' So he's taken to meet God who says, 'Bill, sit down next to me on my right-hand side.'

Al Gore then dies and goes to Heaven, where he's asked who he is and what he did. Al replies, 'I am Al Gore and I was Vice-President of the United States.' So he's taken to meet God who says, 'Al, sit down next to me on my left-hand side.'

Eventually, Hillary Clinton dies and goes to Heaven where she's asked who she is and what she did. Hillary replies, 'I am Hillary Rodham Clinton, wife of the President of the United States.' She's taken to meet God but before he can speak, she says, 'And what are you doing in MY seat?'

Why was it so difficult for Clinton to fire Monica Lewinsky?

He couldn't give her a pink slip without asking her to try it on first.

Chelsea Clinton is feeling ill at college. The head of the college tells her she will telephone her mother. 'Don't do that,' says Chelsea. 'My mother's too busy. Ring my father.'

What's the difference between Bill Clinton and a gigolo?

A gigolo only screws one person at a time.

Bill Clinton was walking along the beach when he saw a bottle in the sand. He kicked it and a genie came out. 'Thank you,' said the genie. 'I've been trapped in this bottle for 500 years.

By way of my appreciation, I will grant you one wish. What would you like?'

'I would like to go down in history,' said Clinton, 'so I'd like to be able to bring peace to the Middle East.'

'I'm afraid there are some things that are just impossible to do,' said the genie. 'Could you come up with another wish?'

Clinton thought for a while and then said, 'Could you make Hillary popular with the American people?'

'Let me have a look at a map of the Middle East,' said the genie.

Why is Bill Clinton a model President?
Because, like a model, he's a small imitation of the real thing.

Dan Quayle was a heartbeat away from the presidency but Al Gore is an orgasm away from the presidency.

Bill Clinton goes to a hair stylist. 'Good morning, Mr President. What are you going to do about Monica Lewinsky?'

'I'm here to have my hair cut, what the hell business is it of yours?'

'I don't care a fuck about her, darling, but it's easier to cut your hair when it stands on end.'

After five years spending millions of dollars, Whitewater investigator Kenneth Starr has finally found the smoking gun – it's inside Clinton's pants.

Clinton's latest statement on the Lewinsky affair has just been released: 'I would never ask anyone to lie. Lie down, maybe, but never lie.'

Bill is known for his love of junk food – and for telling lies. Apparently Burger King is cashing in on the two and is placing a sign on the White House lawn saying: 'Billions of Whoppers Told'.

The good news is that Clinton is going to tell the truth about all his infidelity on live TV. The bad news is that the TV programme is only on for thirty minutes.

Bill hasn't appointed a new Supreme Court judge yet because Hillary hasn't made up her mind.

What's the only election promise that Clinton has kept?
Reuniting Fleetwood Mac.

How can you tell when Bill Clinton is deep in thought?
He takes the 'out to lunch' sign off his head.

How can you tell if Bill Clinton is lying?
His mouth is open.

What is Monica Lewinsky's favourite instrument?
She plays the guitar but she sucks on the organ.

When she was younger, Chelsea Clinton asked her dad if all fairy tales started with the words 'Once upon a time'. 'No,' said, Bill, 'some start with the words "After I'm elected…"'

What do Jeffrey Dahmer's victims and the Clintons' hair-styles have in common?
They both look like the work of a butcher.

Bill Clinton went to his interior decorator one day and said, 'Chelsea has been complaining about her room being ugly. In fact, she said that she doesn't even want to live in it any more. Please take care of it immediately!' The interior decorator replied, 'I'll have those mirrors removed this minute.'

What's the difference between Bill Clinton and a gang-banger?
A gang-banger screws in turn; Bill Clinton screws interns.

Why doesn't Bill Clinton want to go to the movies?
Because he's afraid the usherette will ask to see his stub.

Why is Hillary suing Bill for divorce?
Because he's doing to the country what he should only be doing to her.

Hillary Clinton is, of course, the First Lady. But she sure as hell isn't the last ...

What happens when Bill Clinton is twenty points ahead in the polls?
He can start dating again.

How can you tell Bill Clinton from a bunch of dead bodies?
He's the stiff one.

How many Bill Clintons does it take to change a light bulb?
He doesn't. He whines a while, says 'I feel your pain', gets Congress to pass a multi-million-dollar light security bill, and blames

special interests for not making light bulbs free.

How did Bill and Hillary Clinton meet?
They were dating the same girl in high school.

How can you tell when Bill Clinton is lying?
Only a Bill Clinton supporter is too dumb not to know the answer to this one.

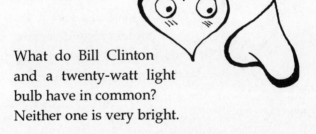

What do Bill Clinton
and a twenty-watt light
bulb have in common?
Neither one is very bright.

What did Clinton do to lose weight?
Ran away from the draft.

Clinton and Nixon share the same nickname – Tricky Dick.

Why is Bill Clinton called a 'middle-of-the-road Democrat'?
Because he's got a wide yellow stripe down the middle of his back.

Bill Clinton gets a letter from a man who says he'll break his legs if he ever bothers his wife again. Clinton goes to his Chief of Staff and asks him what he ought to do. 'OK,' says the aide, 'here's what we do. You've got to contact the man and promise never to see his wife again.'

'That would be fine,' replies Clinton, 'but the trouble is the guy didn't sign his name.'

If Bill and Hillary jumped together off the Washington Monument, who would land first?
Who cares?

Why does Chelsea look so damn stupid and ugly?
Heredity.

What do Clinton and JFK have in common?
They haven't had any brains for the last thirty years.

Who's the odd one out between Dan Quayle, Bill Clinton and Jane Fonda?
Jane Fonda – because she went to Vietnam.

How many Clinton White House officials does it take to change a light bulb?
None. They like to keep him in the dark.

Why was Hillary so interested in Whitewater? She heard whitewater could be found going over a dyke.

Clinton is the only man who can turn attention away from one sex scandal – with ANOTHER sex scandal.

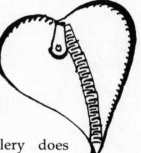

What kind of jewellery does Hillary look best in?
Handcuffs.

Monica Lewinsky's lawyer says she is under so much pressure her back is to the wall. She must be expecting Bill Clinton to come over ...

Why is Chelsea Clinton a miracle child?
Because lawyers always use their personalities for birth control.

Why can't Bill Clinton file a defamation of character suit against his critics?
Because Bill Clinton has no character to defame.

What did Bill Clinton say to promote his inauguration pasties?
'My balls are for everyone.'

What's the best way to kill Clinton?
Give him something that reads: DO NOT INHALE.

How could you prove that the guy who attacked the White House with a plane was insane?
He thought Clinton would be at home in his own bedroom at night.

What did Clinton say when Paula Jones told her story?

'I told her to "do my erection", not "ruin my re-election".'

Apparently, Bill Clinton wants to change the name of the Oval Office to the Oral Office.

What's the difference between the Panama Canal and Hillary Clinton?

One's a busy ship-filled ditch and the other's a dizzy shit-filled bitch.

Why doesn't Bill Clinton like old houses?

He's afraid of the draft.

What's the difference between Bill Clinton and an elephant?

About forty pounds and a sun-tan.

What happened when Bill Clinton was given a shot of testosterone?
He turned into Hillary.

How can you tell if Bill Clinton's had sex with a woman?
He'll deny having met her three months later.

When will there be a woman in the White House?
As soon as Hillary leaves.

What's the difference between Bill Clinton and a pot of yogurt?
Yogurt has culture.

What's the best thing that ever came out of Arkansas?
Highway 55.

What's the new use they found for sheep in Arkansas?
Wool.

What's the difference between Bill Clinton and a whale?
A whale mates for life.

What do you get when you cross a lesbian and a gay?
Chelsea Clinton.

Why did Clinton choose Canada for his summit with Yeltsin?
So he could look up some college buddies who moved up there during the Vietnam War.

Eventually, Hillary berated Bill about his relationship with Monica Lewinsky. 'Aw hell, honey,' said Bill, 'it was only platonic.'

'How so?' asked Hillary suspiciously. 'It was play for her and a tonic for me.'

Why is Clinton always losing his voice?
He keeps having to eat his words.

Why are female White House staff annoyed with Hillary?
She keeps leaving the toilet seat up.

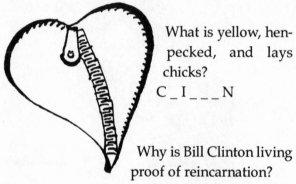

What is yellow, hen-pecked, and lays chicks?
C _ I _ _ _ N

Why is Bill Clinton living proof of reincarnation?
Because no one could get this dumb in one lifetime.

What's the difference between Bill Clinton and Santa Claus?
Some people still believe in Santa Claus.

What's the difference between Bush's Army and Clinton's Army?
Bush's soldiers got blown *out* of fox holes.

What's Bill Clinton's biggest wish?
That someone would wave a hand at him showing more than one finger.

Why is Bill Clinton like a passenger restraint device?
He's a bag of air that isn't on the driver's side.

Bill Clinton's popularity has been declining. In fact, Paula Jones now claims she never met him.

What's the difference between Clinton's health care plan and a kidney stone?
A kidney stone is easier to pass.

What is Hillary's new nickname after her latest hairstyle?
Oldielocks

How can you tell Bill Clinton apart from a cow?
By the wise look in the animal's eyes.

What do you get when you cross Bill Clinton and James Dean?
A man without a clue.

How is the Clinton cabinet like a bowl of Granola?
What isn't fruit and nuts is flakes.

Why does Hillary Clinton wear turtleneck sweaters?
So we can't see her Adam's apple move when Bill talks.

What did Boris Yelstin reply when he was asked if meeting Clinton had made him want to convert Russia to an American style of government?
'Hell no, I'm not going to let my wife run the country.'

It's doubtful that President Clinton will ever be convicted of any of these sex-related charges. There's little chance that the special prosecutor will ever be able to get the evidence to stand up in court.

Why did a Bill Clinton send an unsigned cheque for $1,000 to charity?
He wanted to make an anonymous contribution.

What did Hillary say to Bill before the election?
'We'd better win this one, or I'm moving in with k d lang.'

The big problem with Clinton's new military is that the only way to get promoted is to suck up.

Bill Clinton was asked about his views on euthanasia. 'Youth in Asia,' he replied, 'are just like kids everywhere else.'

How are Boris Becker and President Clinton alike?
Both aren't so successful when they're not on grass.

Bill Clinton has met the devil, but he didn't in hell.

Bill Clinton plans to reduce the budget deficit by an appeal to sacrifice. The problem, however, is that every time he gets near a virgin ...

Hillary stopped using her maiden name when she found out from Monica who the real Rodman was.

Bumper Sticker: IF CLINTON WAS THE ANSWER, IT MUST HAVE BEEN A REAL STUPID QUESTION!

Who did you vote for in the last election?
I voted for Roosevelt
Roosevelt wasn't running last year
Neither was Hillary, but she's running the country

The definition of 'Elixir':
1. A cure-all; a medicine.
2. How Bill Clinton screens any intern at the White House.

In a *Washington Post* poll, 1,000 women were asked if they would sleep with Clinton.
Eighty-two per cent responded: 'Not again.'

Why is Bill Clinton not circumcised?
It would have involved throwing away the best part.

How is Bill like a character actor?
When he shows character, he's acting.

What are the two worst things about Bill Clinton?
His face.

Bill told Hillary that he was tired of always being in the public eye. 'Why don't we take a break then?' she said. 'I've heard of this place in Maryland near the ocean where we can go in disguise and be as anonymous as we like.' So they both got into disguise and went in a cheap car to the spot where Hillary had talked about. They sat there for a while in the car, talking and looking at the ocean and then they got down to some kissing and cuddling. Just when they were getting down to the nitty-gritty, a police officer shone a torch into the car and asked Bill for his ID. 'Please don't arrest me,' said Bill, 'I ain't never done anything like this before.'

'I'm not so bothered about you, Sir,' said the police officer, 'but this woman with you comes here everyday.'

Monica Lewinsky's got a new job. She's going to be Director of the Head Start Program.

Why did the IRS audit Bill Clinton?
Because he listed himself as head of the household.

In the White House, you can not only get AIDS
from sex, but you can also get sex from aides.

What's Clinton's favourite instrument?
The strumpet.

Has the Clinton Presidency been blown?
Well, he's certainly been brought to his knees.

To be fair to him, Bill Clinton's never tried to fill his administration with 'yes men'.
Instead, he wanted 'yes women' in as many positions as possible.

Where's the best place to photograph Clinton and his Cabinet?
A police lineup

What are Clinton's plans for the military?
To transfer seamen to all branches of the armed forces.

What do the Zippergate and Watergate scandals have in common?
Deep Throats.

It's only fitting that Bill Clinton gave Monica Lewinsky a hair pin as a gift. All he ever sees of her is the top of her head.

What's Clinton's favorite instrument?
The sex-a-phone.

What do Bill Clinton and Kurt Cobain have in common?
Half a brain and Gore on their backs.

George Bush reminded many women of their husbands. Bill Clinton reminds many women why an increasing number of them are staying single.

Most Americans think it's outrageous that a man of Bill Clinton's age is getting sex from a 21-year-old. However, he did get a nice phone call from Woody Allen.

No President has brought pleasure to as many Americans as Bill Clinton. And that's only counting the interns.

Congress has launched an enquiry into the Lewinsky affair and has put Lorena Bobbitt in charge. Lorena is known for getting to the 'root' of the problem.

Bumper sticker on Arkansan car: IF YOU CAN READ THIS, YOU'RE NOT FROM HERE.

The Clintons are running a rock and roll presidency: It ain't working, Hilary wants our money for nothing and Bill gets his chicks for free.

Apparently, the Secret Service code word for Bill Clinton has been changed from Jogger to 'Mr Mom'.

Bill Clinton called up Ray McVeigh after the Oklahoma bombing and asked if they could meet. But McVeigh said he couldn't afford the bad publicity.

Bumper Sticker: CLINTON HAPPENS.

What's the difference between Bill Clinton and Saddam Hussein?
One's a screwball who lies to the world and the other's the leader of Iraq

What's the difference between Bill Clinton and a pig?
One's got its nose permanently in the trough and the other lives in a farmyard.

The Chrysler Corporation is adding a new car to its line in honour of Bill Clinton. It's going to be called the Dodge Draft.

Bill Clinton was asked what he thought about foreign affairs. 'I don't know,' he replied, 'I never had one.'

Bill Clinton intends to go down in history – as the most hands-on President ...

The last inauguration went without a hitch, but apparently it took three secret service agents to hold Hillary's hand down during the swearing-in ceremony.

When Clinton was asked about Roe v Wade, he replied, 'I think the Cubans had better row because it's too far to wade.'

If fifty per cent of adults are illiterate, how come Bill Clinton only got forty-three per cent of the vote?

Bill Clinton's mother prayed fervently that her son would grow up and be President.
So far, only half of her prayer has been answered.

They're now marketing Bill Clinton golf balls. They don't fly straight, but they give you a great lie.

Why is Bill Clinton like railroad track?
He's been laid all over the country.

If character isn't an issue now, why isn't Ted Kennedy President?

What's Clinton's favourite instrument?
The whore-monica.

Definition of an oxymoron: Clinton character assassination.

Bill Clinton is so fat that when he wears his yellow raincoat, people shout, 'Taxi!'

President Clinton's got a new promise: 'Smell my lips ... No more Bush.'

It's election night and Bill Clinton says to his wife, 'Well, Honey, we won!'
    'Honestly?' asks Hillary.
    'Let's not go too far,' says Bill.

The trouble with political jokes is that they get elected President.

Four doctors – a Frenchman, a German, an Italian and an American – are discussing medicine at an international medical convention. The Frenchman says, 'medicine in France is so advanced that we can put a new heart in a man and have him looking for work in five weeks.'

The German says, 'That's nothing. In Germany we can put a new lung in a man and have him looking for work in four weeks.'

The Italian says, 'That's nothing. In Italy, we can put a new liver in a man and have him looking for work in three weeks.'

The American doctor smiles and says, 'You guys don't know nothing. We can take an arsehole out of Arkansas, put him in the White House, and the very next day half the country is out there looking for work!'

Chelsea asks Hillary: 'What did you have at the state dinner?'

'Some chicken, some broccoli and 7,374 green peas,' replies Hillary.

'When did you count the peas, Mom?'

'While your father was giving his speech.'

Bill Clinton is a truly composite president. He has the hormones of John F Kennedy, the scruples of Richard Nixon and the memory of Ronald Reagan.

Bumper Sticker: YOU CAN'T SHIT HERE BECAUSE YOUR ASSHOLE'S IN THE WHITE HOUSE.

Hamas has just claimed credit for an act of terrorism against all US citizens. They didn't try to kill Bill Clinton when he went to the Middle East.

How did Bill Clinton get a crick in his neck?
When he was trying to save both faces.

At a recent press conference, Mr Clinton gave his verdict on the world's trouble spots:
Beirut: 'A great ball player, but Hank Aaron hit more homers.'
Red China: 'Looks great with a white table cloth.'

Why doesn't Hillary wear mini-skirts in the White House?
Because she doesn't want people to see her balls.

Bill Clinton's out horseriding and he hears someone shout, 'Hey, look at the prick on that horse!' When he gets back home, he gets off the horse and sees he's been riding a mare.

What do bands play at official presidential functions?
Don't Inhale to the Chief.

What's the difference between Hillary Clinton and a pit bull?
The pit bull doesn't carry a briefcase.

What was Bill Clinton's favourite war song? 'Over Here'.

Hillary walked into her bedroom with a big smile. 'How come you're in such a good mood?' asked Bill.

'I just got back from my annual medical,' replied Hillary, 'and the doctor said I had the breasts of a thirty-year-old woman.'

'Did he say anything about your fifty-year-old arse?'

'No,' said Hillary, 'your name wasn't even mentioned.'

Clinton is out jogging in one of the seedier areas of Washington, DC when he bumps into a prostitute. She says, 'OK, buddy, it's $50 for sex.' Bill's tempted but the price is too high, so he asks her if she'll take five. Disgusted, the tart walks off and Bill continues his run. A few days later, he's out jogging again in the same area and encounters the same prostitute.

However, she still won't go down from fifty to five. A week later, Bill is accompanied on his run by Hillary who's trying to get into shape, and once again the same prostitute is still there. She looks at Bill and Hillary together and says, 'Now you see what you get for five dollars?'

What have Bill Clinton and Saddam Hussein got in common?
They won't let experts examine their secret weapon.

Bumper Sticker: I'M GLAD I'M AN AMERICAN, I'M GLAD I'M FREE. I WISH I WAS A DOG AND CLINTON WAS A TREE.

Bill Clinton is considering changing the Democratic Party emblem from a donkey to a condom, because it stands for inflation, gives a false sense of security and protects a prick.

While Bill, Hillary and Chelsea were having a vacation at Camp David, their housekeeper at the White House was charged with looking after their pet parrot. They hadn't been gone for more than a day when the parrot died. The housekeeper knew that the Clintons would be inconsolable at the loss of their parrot, so she set out to find a replacement. She visited nearly every pet store in Washington before she found a sufficiently similar bird. However, as she was buying the parrot, the shop owner warned her that the bird had previously been owned by a Madam and had lived for several years in a brothel. The housekeeper was so relieved at finding a suitable bird that she decided to buy it anyway. When the Clintons returned to the White House, Chelsea walked into the room first and the bird said, 'Too young'. Then in walked Hillary and the bird said, 'Too old'. Finally, the President entered the room and the bird shouted out, 'Hi, Bill, how're you doing?'

Bumper Sticker: IT'S STILL THE ECONOMY.
AND HE'S STILL STUPID.

Hillary is being driven around Washington, DC when she spots a little boy sitting in a park with a cart. Thinking of the PR possibilities, she asks her driver to pull over. She gets out and notices that the little boy has five little kittens in his cart. She says how much she likes them and the little boy says, 'Thank you, they're Democrats!' Hillary is, naturally enough, thrilled by this. A few days later, she goes back to the park with a film crew. When they come across the little boy, Hillary asks after the kittens. 'They're fine,' says the boy, 'they're Republicans.'

'Wait a minute,' says Hillary, 'you told me they were Democrats.'

'Ah yes,' replied the boy, 'but now their eyes are open.'

What's the difference between Air Force One and a porcupine?
A porcupine has pricks on the outside.

When Bill comes up with a law, it's a joke, but when Hillary comes up with a joke, it's the law.

People say Hillary is big-headed but it's not true. Recently, after a hectic day of hand-shaking in the capital, Bill collapsed on to the marital bed and gasped, 'God, I'm tired.' Hillary looked at him with a withering eye, 'I've told you before – in the privacy of the bedroom it's perfectly acceptable to call me Hillary.'

Chelsea asks Bill: 'Daddy, what's a lesbian?' 'Ask Mummy, he'll show you.'

Boris Yeltsin invited Bill Clinton to go and watch the Moscow May Day parade. The parade started with a division of infantry, followed by armoured personnel carriers, tanks and artillery. During the parade there were squadrons of aeroplanes flying overhead.

Clinton, who had never been so close to war in his life, was incre-dibly impressed. Then he noticed that, at the back of the parade, there were a few men in suits.

'Who are those guys?' he asked Yeltsin.

'Those are the economists,' replied the Russian leader.

'But I thought this was a military parade,' said Clinton.

'Ah,' said Yeltsin, 'but have you seen the damage that they can do?'

Which is the odd one out between a Clinton Administration official who tells the truth, a Clinton Administration official who always lies, and the Tooth Fairy?
The Clinton Administration official who always lies (because the other two don't exist).

Which is the odd one out between AIDS, herpes and Bill Clinton?
Bill Clinton – it only *seems* like he lasts forever.

What were Bill's two favourite campaign promises?
'The cheque's in your mouth' and 'I won't come in the post'.

What's Clinton's favourite baseball team?
The Dodgers.

Why did Monica always get on top?
Because Bill can only fuck up.

Clinton is shaking hands with the people. 'I'm pleased to meet you,' says a man to the President, 'I've heard a lot about you.' Clinton laughs nervously, 'But can you prove any of it?'

Why do they always take a live turkey on Air Force One?
For spare parts.

Why is it more dangerous to sit next to a smoking Bill Clinton than it is to sit next to any other smoker?
Clinton's smoke is still firsthand.

Bumper Sticker: CLINTON DOESN'T INHALE, HE SUCKS!

Why is Bill Clinton diverting federal funds from improving schools to improving jails?
Because when his Presidency is through, he won't be going to school.

Bumper Sticker: FIRST GENNIFER, THEN MONICA, NOW US.

Clinton is merely doing for gays in the military what Hillary has in the White House. As long as she doesn't tell anyone she's the President, she can continue to be the President.

Why does the secret service guard Hillary so closely?
Because if anything happens to her, Bill becomes President.

Bill Clinton had heard of all the starving people in Somalia and wanted to take a look for himself. On the plane there, the president looked down with his binoculars, and said, 'Hell, look at them! Skinny, starving, what are we going to do about it?' At which point, an aide said, 'Er, Mr President, that's not Somalia. That's Arkansas.'

What has two wings and a crooked willie?
Air Force One.

If he's called to testify in a trial, how soon will Clinton commit perjury?
When he's sworn in.

Here's the real reason why Clinton got himself that dog Buddy. It's so that whenever Hillary walks past his office, she won't be surprised to hear him saying, 'Sit, lie down, roll over. Now, here's your bone ...'

Why does Hillary Clinton have crow's feet around her eyes?
From constantly squinting when she says 'Suck what?'

Why did Bill Clinton cross the road?
To meet the chick.

Bumper Sticker: IMPEACH CLINTON! AND
HER HUSBAND TOO!

What do Hillary Clinton and Gerald Ford have
in common?
They've both been President without being
elected.

What does Hillary Clinton do with her
arsehole every morning?
She puts a suit and tie on him and sends him
off to work.

For which Arkansas State Supreme Court deci-
sion is Hillary Clinton famous?
If you divorce your wife in Arkansas, is she
still your cousin?

How does Bill Clinton say 'Fuck you'?
'Trust me.'

What does Bill say to
Hillary before having sex?
'Honey, I'll be home in forty
minutes.'

What does Bill say to Hillary
after having sex?
'You'd better pick me up
before she calls the cops.'

What will Clinton do for the Navy?
Give the position of Rear Admiral a new
meaning.

Why did Chelsea grow up confused?
Because her father couldn't keep his pants on
and her mother always wanted to wear them.

What is Clinton's plan to create thousands of small businesses?
Take thousands of big businesses and wait for two years.

Why was Bill angry with Chelsea's private school?
They broke family tradition by making her wear a uniform.

What has Clinton done that no one has been able to do in the last ten years?
Unite the Republican Party.

When did Clinton's friends know for sure that he had political ambitions?
When he married out of his family.

What does Bill Clinton have in common with the great Presidents?
Absolutely nothing.

What do you get when you give Bill Clinton a penny for his thoughts?
Change.

What do Bill Clinton and the Mississippi River have in common?
Both are wet, meander all over the place, and are controlled by dykes.

For Bill Clinton's girlfriends sex is like a pretzel: twisted and salty.

What's Bill Clinton's girlfriends' favourite nursery rhyme?
Humpme Dumpme.

What does Clinton need to stop the white water?
A water gate.

What does David Koresh have in common with Bill Clinton?
They smoked but didn't inhale.

How is Bill Clinton like an unemployed schoolteacher?
He's got no class and no principals.

What's the difference between Bill Clinton and a pickpocket?
A pickpocket snatches watches.

What do Hillary Clinton and the city of Buffalo have in common?
They both have Bills that are losers.

What's the difference between Hillary Clinton and the Scottish oil fields?
The Scottish oil fields get drilled once in a while.

If you had Clinton, Gore and Dolly Parton on stage together, what would you have?
Two boobs and a country singer

What's the difference between President Hoover and Clinton?
One promised a chicken in every pot and the other was a chicken who smoked pot.

What was Clinton's very first executive order?
Flowers by the bedside.

A man goes into a bar in the Mid-West and orders a beer. On the bar's TV is Bill Clinton. The man says out loud, 'What a horse's arse!' and is amazed when the man sitting next to him punches him in the face. 'Hey,' says the man nursing his jaw, 'are you some kind of Clinton supporter?'

'Hell no,' says his assailant, 'I just love horses.'

Bill and Hillary Clinton and Al Gore were in the Presidential helicopter, flying over Washington, DC when Bill said, 'I'm going to throw a one hundred dollar bill out the window and make someone down there happy.'

Hillary said, 'Why don't you throw out two fifty dollar bills and make two people happy?'

Then Al Gore said, 'Why don't you throw five twenty dollar bills out and make five people happy?'

At this point, the helicopter pilot turned round and said, 'Why don't I throw all three of you out and make the whole country happy?'

During the 1996 presidential election, there was a poll putting Clinton and Dole in a dead heat. It turned out to be a mistake: Dole was dead and Clinton was in heat.

It's winter and Bill Clinton is walking on the White House lawn, when he finds a message written in the snow saying, 'Clinton is a pig'. Furious about this, he calls in the CIA to look into the matter. The next day, the CIA boss reports back to the President that they've got bad news, 'The message was written in urine, sir.'

'That's terrible,' says Clinton.

'It's worse than that,' replies the CIA chief, 'the urine belongs to Al Gore.'

'I don't believe it!' cries Clinton.

'It's even worse than that,' says the CIA chief, 'It's written in Hillary's handwriting.'

Why do they put Bill Clinton's picture on the insides of toilet bowls?
So the arseholes can see who they voted for.

What do you get when you cross Bill Clinton with an Italian?
A waiter who won't serve.

One morning, Bill Clinton was out having a jog with a few of his Secret Service Agents. After a few miles, Bill says to one of the agents, 'When I get home, I'm going to rip off Hillary's panties.'

'Are you feeling a little sexy today, Sir?'

'No,' replies Bill, 'it's just that the damn things keep cutting in to me!'

Why does Bill Clinton always take Hillary with him wherever he goes?
So he doesn't have to kiss her goodbye.

Bill Clinton is deep in prayer. 'Lord,' he asks, 'why did you make women so beautiful?'

'So that you would like them, my son.'

'Lord, why did you make women so sexy?'

'So that you would like them, my son.'

'Lord, why did you make them so stupid?'

'So that they would like you, my son.'

Why won't there be a White House Christmas pageant this year?

They can't find three wise men and a virgin.

Why wouldn't a shark bite Hillary Clinton?

Professional courtesy.

Bill Clinton's home state of Arkansas has the lowest teen pregnancy rate in the nation.
Lucky that Bill always wore a condom.

Why do people in Arkansas have peanut butter and jelly for Thanksgiving?
Because they sent their turkey to the White House.

Bill asks out a White House secretary. 'Mr President,' says the secretary, 'if you can raise my skirt as high as you've raised our taxes, if you can get your dick as hard as you've made our lives, if you can screw me like you've screwed the American people, then it would be my pleasure to go out with you.'

How did Bill Clinton paralyse Hillary from the waist down?
He married her.

Bill Clinton, Al Gore and Dan Quayle are in a boat when it suddenly starts leaking. They have only one lifejacket. Bill says: 'Let's do the Democratic thing. Let's vote to see who gets the lifejacket.' They each write a name on a piece of paper. Gore and Quayle get one vote each. Clinton gets four.

Bill Clinton was on Air Force One when the stewardess served him a drink. 'Here's something new,' she said, 'an ice cube with a hole in it.'

'Ain't nothing knew,' said Bill, 'I've been married to one for years.'

Did you hear that Bill Clinton got thrown out of the Boy Scouts? Apparently he was eating Brownies.

Bill Clinton told Hillary that he needed more space. So she locked him out of the White House.

Bill Clinton went into the confessional booth at his local Catholic church and told the priest, 'Father, I had six women last night.'

'What sort of Catholic are you, my son?' said the shocked priest.

'Oh hell, I ain't no Catholic,' said Bill, 'but I sure had to tell someone.'

Why does Bill always keep the lights on during sex?

So he doesn't call out the wrong name.

What's the difference between Hillary Clinton and a terrorist?

A terrorist doesn't make so many demands.

What's the only thing that is less exciting than hearing Bill Clinton speak?

Watching Hillary Clinton undress.

What's the difference between 'vision' and 'sight'?
Claudia Schiffer is a vision; Hillary Clinton is a sight.

What's Bill Clinton's definition of infidelity?
Not looking in the mirror.

What's the difference between Hillary Clinton and a hound?
Lipstick.

Why does Bill Clinton lie with a straight face?
So that he can lie with a curved body.

Bill Clinton was tired of his public image so he called up the head of the CIA and asked him to send over his best agent. The next day the agent arrived at the White House. 'I understand you're the best agent in the CIA,' said Bill, 'so I want you to go all over the country and find out what Americans really want from their President.' The agent agreed and went off. Four months later, he reappeared at the White House. 'Well,' said Bill, 'did you find out what the American people want?'

'Yes, I did,' replied the agent.

'Please let me know what the people want,' said Bill. So the agent pulled out his gun and shot the President.

It was so cold last winter that Bill and Hillary actually slept together, just to keep warm.

What's Bill Clinton's idea of foreplay?
'Yo, look at this, bitch!'

New on the market: the Hillary Clinton inflatable sex doll. Just fill it with ice water and she's ready to go.

Maybe Bill Clinton isn't guilty after all. Everyone thought Richard Jewell was guilty of planting the bomb at the Atlanta Olympics and he turned out to be innocent. But can you really compare Jewell with Clinton? One's a reviled idiot, the other's a respected security guard.

Why is the Clinton White House like a wet dream?
They're both coming unscrewed.

What do you get if you cross Hillary Clinton and a gorilla?
Nothing. There are some things that even a gorilla won't do.

What's special about the lift in the White House?
It's the only thing that Hillary Clinton ever goes down on.

Why is Bill Clinton's penis really burning?
Because people keep talking about it.

Apparently, Bill Clinton is an insomniac, an agnostic and a dyslexic. That's right. He stays up all night wondering if there's a dog.

Apparently we've been doing Bill Clinton a disservice. He didn't ask Monica Lewinsky to lie under deposition, he asked her to 'lie in this position'.

The US Post Office was thinking of issuing stamps with Bill and Hillary's faces on them. Unfortunately, test marketing showed that people would spit on the wrong side of the stamps.

A reporter asked Bill Clinton what he thought of Babe Ruth. Clinton replied, 'He's my hero.' The reporter decided to tackle him on this: 'Sir, do you think it's right that the President of the United States should have as his hero a beer-drinking, womanizing, partying baseball player?'

'What?' said Bill, 'He played baseball?'.

Bill Clinton is visiting a Washington school. In one class, he asks the children if anyone can give him an example of a TRAGEDY. One boy stands up and says, 'If my best friend was playing in the street and a car came along and killed him, then that would be a TRAGEDY.'

'No,' says Clinton, 'that would be an ACCIDENT.'

Another boy offers a definition: 'If a school bus carrying forty children drove off a cliff, that would be a TRAGEDY.'

'No,' says Clinton, 'that would be a GREAT LOSS.'

The room goes silent as none of the other children can think of what to say. 'Come on,' says Clinton, 'isn't there anyone here who can give me an example of a TRAGEDY?'

Finally, a boy raises his hand and says, 'If an aeroplane carrying the President and the First Lady crashed, that would be a TRAGEDY.'

'That's absolutely right,' says a delighted Clinton. 'Now please tell the rest of the class why that would indeed be a TRAGEDY.'

'Well,' says the boy, 'it wouldn't be an ACCIDENT and it sure as hell wouldn't be no GREAT LOSS.'

And, finally, just in case Teddy's feeling left out:

Why do Kennedys cry during sex?
Mace.

Why did Ted Kennedy spend four hours in the voting booth?
He thought he was in a confessional.

What do you call someone who sees the glass in front of him as half full?
An optimist.
What do you call someone who sees the glass in front of him as half empty?
Ted Kennedy